World Wisd
The Library of Perenn

The Library of Perennial Philosophy is dedicated to the timeless Truth underlying the diverse religions. This Truth, often referred to as the *Sophia Perennis*—or Perennial Wisdom—finds its expression in the revealed Scriptures as well as the writings of the great sages and the artistic creations of the traditional worlds.

Spirit of the Indian Warrior appears as one of our selections in the Sacred Worlds series.

Sacred Worlds Series

The Sacred Worlds series blends images of visual beauty with focused selections from the writings of the great religions of the world, including both scripture and the writings of the sages and saints. Books in the Sacred Worlds series may be based upon a particular religious tradition, or upon a universal religious theme such as prayer or virtue.

Praise for the Sacred Worlds Series

"[This series] combines impressive imagery—both new and old fine arts, as well as contemporary and vintage photography—with selections from world faith traditions. . . . These entries in the 'Sacred Worlds' series are delights to the eye and the mind."
—Library Journal

Battle of the Little Bighorn,
by Amos Bad Heart Bull,
Sioux, late 1800s or early 1900s

About the Series Editors

"One of the great callings of art is to excavate a lost part of our culture, and the Fitzgeralds answer this summons handsomely here in a compact exploration of Native American women's spirituality."
   —Publishers Weekly on *The Spirit of Indian Women*

"*The Spirit of Indian Women* . . . is an act of reclamation as much as of spirituality: it reproduces precious and seldom-seen photographs of Native American women. . . . Their images are interwoven with oral accounts, songs, and other documents that offer priceless glimpses into the little-understood lives and experiences of America's foremothers. . . . *The Spirit of Indian Women* is a special treasure. Highly recommended."
   —Library Journal

"[*World of the Teton Sioux Indians*] is effectively edited by Joseph A. Fitzgerald to facilitate its reading and allow the lay reader to enjoy the discovery, depth, and meaning of tribal culture and the songs that were handed down from time immemorial."
   —Charles Trimble, former Executive Director of the American Indian Press Association, author of *Iyeska*

"Michael Fitzgerald has heard the poignant narratives of the American Indian people, and has lived among the Crow people for extended periods of time since 1970. . . . We thank Fitzgerald for his deep-seated appreciation, honor, and respect for American Indian culture, its religion, language, and lifeways."
   —Janine Pease, founding president of the Little Big Horn College, and National Indian Educator of the Year

"My son, Michael Fitzgerald, has been a member of my family and the Crow tribe for over twenty years. Michael has helped to preserve the spiritual traditions of the Crow Sun Dance and he has helped to show us the wisdom of the old-timers."
   —Thomas Yellowtail, Crow Medicine Man and Sun Dance Chief

"I greatly appreciate the recovery work that Fitzgerald is doing, work that makes available for the classroom and popular use texts that have been all but buried in libraries. Work such as Fitzgerald's is exactly the kind of work that needs to be promoted for a more complete understanding of early American Indian writings and oratory."
   —Stephen Brandon, University of New Mexico

"The quotations [of *Spirit of the Earth* are] . . . so well chosen, so well paired with the images, and so beautifully centered on our appreciation, understanding, and lasting reliance on the natural world, they do what our traditional stories have always done—engage and teach."
   —Joseph Bruchac, author of *Keepers of the Earth, Code Talker: A Book About the Navajo Marines*, and *Crazy Horse's Vision*

SPIRIT OF THE INDIAN WARRIOR

+ + +

Edited by

MICHAEL OREN FITZGERALD

&

JOSEPH A. FITZGERALD

Foreword by
CHARLES TRIMBLE

World Wisdom

Spirit of the Indian Warrior
© 2019 World Wisdom, Inc.

Library of Congress Cataloging-in-Publication Data

Names: Fitzgerald, Michael Oren, 1949- editor. | Fitzgerald, Joseph A., 1977-
editor. | Trimble, Charles E., writer of foreword.
Title: Spirit of the Indian warrior / edited by Michael Oren Fitzgerald &
Joseph A. Fitzgerald ; foreword by Charles Trimble.
Description: Bloomington, Inidana : World Wisdom, [2019] | Series: Sacred
worlds series | Includes bibliographical references. |
Identifiers: LCCN 2018053120 (print) | LCCN 2019004367 (ebook) | ISBN
9781936597635 (epub) | ISBN 9781936597628 (pbk. : alk. paper)
Subjects: LCSH: Speeches, addresses, etc., American–Indian authors. |
Indians of North America–Quotations. | Values. | Spirituality.
Classification: LCC E98.O7 (ebook) | LCC E98.O7 S65 2019 (print) | DDC
970.004/97–dc23
LC record available at https://url.emailprotection.link/?aQIGj4lOvUgMGIEdjJ2U_
yBIxGWhXBRj89w538IOjiQs~

Front cover: Heebe-tee-tse, Shoshone, 1899.
Photograph by Rose & Hopkins

Back cover: Two Warriors, by Amos Bad Heart Bull,
Sioux, late 1800s or early 1900s

Printed on acid-free paper in China.

For information address World Wisdom, Inc.
P.O. Box 2682, Bloomington, Indiana 47402-2682
www.worldwisdom.com

Hoka-Hey!

+ +
+
+ +

"Come on! Charge!"
(Sioux rallying cry)

CONTENTS

THE INDIAN WARRIOR   1

FOREWORD

I was once asked by a non-Indian friend, "Why does every quotation of an Indian war chief or holy man sound like poetry? Did Indians just sit around pondering nature and humankind and uttering profundities?"

The question, asked in jest, is valid nonetheless.

Oratory was an important element of leadership and influence among Indian people and the use of symbolism and metaphor was essential to their oral tradition. This made for quotable expressions that are harvested for anthologies published for a market of appreciative scholars of philosophy, religion, and history, as well as casual readers inspired by such pristine thought.

Throughout history, American Indian tribal leaders have used oration effectively for governance and diplomacy. Tribal affairs were settled without need of the written word, and intertribal conflict was often avoided as well.

This collection, *Spirit of the Indian Warrior*, contains notable observations and speeches by some of history's greatest warriors and tribal leaders. It offers an intimate window into their spirituality, cultural values, and understanding of the tide and time of a brutal history engulfing them.

The many quotes in this book express values of courage, tribal patriotism, loyalty, generosity, and autonomy. Absent are any expressions of braggadocio or bombast, for another value of the warrior was humility. Accounts of brave deeds were given to the village crier by a hero's fellow warriors for reporting to the community and recording in winter counts or storytellers' memory. Bragging was beneath the warrior's status.

Warrior spirituality was manifest in individual rituals, prayers, and death songs in preparation for battle and for a courageous end, should that be his fate. These are also to be found in this volume.

The warrior fought for territorial integrity, and defense against raids from other tribes and, later, against invading American military. The warrior societies of the Great Plains were peace keepers in the village and disciplinarians in maintaining order on the move and on the hunt. Initiation into the societies required adherence to all the values of the culture, especially that of generosity.

Faced with an endless onslaught to take their hunting grounds, and to destroy their cultures and tribal structures in the name of Manifest Destiny, they resisted courageously, often against impossible odds and, over time, with their food sources destroyed and their numbers overwhelmed, they remained noble and forthright, even in surrender.

But hope for the future remains strong among their proud descendants, who continue to keep their tribal nations alive and functioning, and the words of the Indian warrior live on and inspire the people of the First Nations of the American continents, as well as people all over the world.

Charles Trimble

Military funeral of Clayton Gibbons, cousin of the author, who died in 1943. In view is the stone monument marking the mass grave of the men, women, and children massacred at Wounded Knee, South Dakota

PREFACE

"The warriors went on the warpath," Ohiyesa tells us, "for the protection of the tribe and its hunting grounds." The only reward a warrior desired was, in Thayendanegea's words, "the consciousness of having served his nation."

To be a warrior was not, as we will see, limited to men, but it was men primarily who performed this role. Moreover, to continually risk their life on the battlefield was central to their identity. "That is what makes a man: to fight and to be brave," Lone Chief's mother told him at an early age. Without this struggle for life, a man will decline and society will degenerate. "It is not good for people to have an easy life," James Kaywaykla's grandfather tells us, for "every struggle, whether won or lost, strengthens us for the next to come." More directly, a Papago song asks:

> Is it for me to eat what food I have
> And all day sit idle?

A warrior must look suffering and death in the face. "Nothing lives long," sang White Antelope as he faced his own death, "except the earth and the mountains." Or as Little Bear told a young Iron Hawk: "Take courage, boy! The earth is all that lasts!" Life is fleeting and death is a meeting with our Creator. Wooden Leg relates that before battle a man would put on his best clothing, "not from a belief that it will add to the fighting ability" but because he "wants to look his best when he goes to meet the Great Spirit." Likewise, when their village was attacked Iron-bull and Sits-in-the-middle-of-the-land both were telling their fellow warriors: "This is the day to go fighting to your Father."

In defense of their village, or to avenge a loved-one, some women were also warriors. "I am a woman, but I fought for my people," declared Moving Robe, describing her part in the Battle of the Little Bighorn. A Winnebago song tells of another who fought for her people:

> Greatly
> She
> Defending her children
> The old woman
> Fought for us all

Those women who did not fight urged on the men to do so. According to Plenty Coups: "While we painted ourselves the drums kept beating, and our women sang war-songs. No man can feel himself a coward at such a time." And according to Black Elk: "I saw a very pretty young woman among a band of warriors . . . singing like this: 'Brothers now your friends have come! Be brave! Be brave! Would you see me taken captive?'" After the fighting was over, the women also mourned for those who fell, as described in another Winnebago song:

> Is there anyone who
> Would weep for me?
> My wife
> Would weep for me.

If it is true that a warrior might become vindictive or cruel, it is also true that a warrior's generosity was admired and rewarded. "I was appointed a chief," Plenty Coups relates, "for it was considered a brave deed to spare the lives of two enemies." A warrior sought glory—and might boast of glory he won—but as Ohiyesa writes, "it was the degree of risk that brought honor, rather than the number slain."[1] In part because of this, disputes between tribes were, according to Red Jacket, "generally settled without the shedding of much blood."

The first European immigrants to North America, Red Jacket tells us, were treated kindly: "Your forefathers crossed the great waters and landed upon this island. . . . We took pity on them. . . . We gave them corn and meat." "Our seats were once large, and yours were very small," Red Jacket continues, but now after only a short while "we have scarcely a place left to spread our blankets."

In the face of this threat, many Indian warriors and chiefs vowed, like Tecumseh, "to resist as long as I live and breathe." Some sought or accepted treaties of peace, but they soon found, like Chief Joseph, that

---

[1] The stealing of horses was also seen as a deed of no small risk and therefore worthy of honor. And for many tribes, to touch an enemy and escape unharmed—sometimes called "counting coup"—was even more prestigious than to kill an enemy.

Plenty Coups, Crow, c. 1908

these were worth little: "What treaty that the whites have kept has the red man broken? Not one. What treaty that the whites ever made with us red men have they kept? Not one." And so the newcomers continued their territorial expansion.

"The armies of the whites," says Shabonee, "are without number, like the sands of the sea, and ruin will follow all tribes that go to war with them." These words were sadly proven to be true, and all who did not die fighting were ultimately forced to surrender. "My people," Chief Joseph laments "have no blankets, no food. . . . I am tired; my heart is sick and sad. From where the sun now stands, I will fight no more forever."

After their military defeat, the Indians generally suffered harsh treatment by the political and military authorities. Black Hawk wished that others would "never experience the humility that the power of the American Government has reduced me to." Many who surrendered as warriors, were treated as criminals. "If I had known that I would be sent to the penitentiary I would not have surrendered," stated Big Eagle, who knew that he was no murderer and that if he "had killed or wounded a man it had been in fair, open fight."

For some old-timers, the reservation period was seen simply as the end of their former way of life. "Nothing happened after that," states Two Leggings, "no more war parties, no capturing of horses from the Piegans and the Sioux, no buffalo to hunt." But for Plenty Coups, and many others, the traditional values live on in a new setting. "My heart sings with pride," said Plenty Coups, "when I think of the fighting my people, the red men of all tribes, did in this last great war." Plenty Coups is speaking of the First World War, during the first six months of which 12,000 Indian men volunteered to fight. These were joined by 5,000 more over the course of the war, representing the largest *pro rata* military service of any ethnic group.[2] It is a distinction that native peoples hold to this day. This volume ends with photographs of some of the many contemporary armed service men and women who proudly carry on this ancestral tradition.

---

[2] This effort was not limited to service in the military alone: Native communities, despite being among the poorest in America, bought $25 million worth of war bonds during the First World War—$75 for every man, woman, and child. As many as 10,000 American Indian women also joined the Red Cross.

What then is the spirit of the Indian warrior? As seen above, and shown further below, it is to serve as protector of the community, to have courage in the face of danger, to be generous in victory, to keep self-respect in defeat, and to take pride in the heroism of others—it is all of this, and more. Whatever our present circumstances, we can surely all draw inspiration from qualities such as these.

Michael Oren Fitzgerald
Joseph A. Fitzgerald

Grand Entry, Eastern Shoshone Indian Days,
Fort Washakie, Wyoming

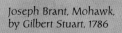
Joseph Brant, Mohawk,
by Gilbert Stuart, 1786

THE INDIAN WARRIOR

IF MY WARRIORS ARE TO FIGHT they are too few; if they are to die they are too many.

Hendrick (Teoniahigarawe), Mohawk

ᴄᴄᴄ

NO PERSON AMONG US desires any other reward for performing a brave and worthy action, but the consciousness of having served his nation.

Joseph Brant (Thayendanegea), Mohawk

ᴄᴄᴄ

GRANDFATHER IMPRESSED UPON ME that every struggle, whether won or lost, strengthens us for the next to come. It is not good for people to have an easy life. They become weak and inefficient when they cease to struggle. Some need a series of defeats before developing the strength and courage to win a victory.

James Kaywaykla, Apache

ᴄᴄᴄ

WHEN I SHOT any kind of bird, when I killed, I saw that its life went out with its blood. This taught me for what purpose I am here. I came into this world to die. My body is only to hold a spirit life. Should my blood be sprinkled, I want no wounds from behind. Death should come fronting me.

Toohoolhoolzote, Nez Pierce

THE INDIAN WARRIOR

Lenape warriors in Union army,
by Jules Worms, 1863

THE INDIAN WARRIOR

THE WARRIORS WENT ON THE WARPATH for the protection of the tribe and its hunting grounds. All the people shared in this benefit, so when the warrior fulfilled his vow he wanted all the tribe to share in its benefits. He believed that Wakan Tanka is more ready to grant the requests of those who make vows and fulfill them than of those who are careless of all their obligations; also that an act performed publicly is more effective than the same thing done privately. So when a man was fulfilling his vow, he prayed for all the members of the tribe and for all the branches of the tribe, wherever they might be.

Red Bird, Sioux

THE ATTITUDE OF THE INDIAN TOWARD DEATH, the test and background of life, is entirely consistent with his character and philosophy. Death has no terror for him; he meets it with simplicity and perfect calm, seeking only an honorable end as his last gift to his family and descendants.

Charles Eastman (Ohiyesa), Sioux

NOW BROTHER, as for me, I assure you I will press on, and though contrary winds may blow strong in my face, yet I will never turn back; but will continue to press forward till I have finished. I would have you do the same.

Teedyuscung, Lenape

3

THE INDIAN WARRIOR

OH SUN! Make this boy strong and brave. May he die in battle rather than from old age or sickness.

Unidentified Blackfoot

I DO NOT WISH to be an old man.
This day is mine to die.

Cheyenne Song

A WARRIOR
I have been.
Now, it is all over.
A hard time
I have.

Sitting Bull's Last Song, Sioux

IN OUR NATURAL STATE, it was the degree of risk that brought honor, rather than the number slain, and a brave man would mourn thirty days, with blackened face and loosened hair, for the enemy whose life had been taken. And while the spoils of war were allowed, this did not extend to appropriation of the other's territory, nor was there any wish to overthrow another nation and enslave its people. Indeed, if an enemy honored us with a call, his trust was not misplaced, and he went away convinced that he had met with a royal host! Our honor was the guarantee for safety, so long as he remained within the camp.

Charles Eastman (Ohiyesa), Sioux

Mountain Chief, Blackfoot, with coup stick and carved horse representing war deeds, 1909

Red Jacket, Seneca,
by George Catlin, 1827

THE INDIAN WARRIOR

IF WE HAD ANY DISPUTES about hunting grounds, they were generally settled without the shedding of much blood. But an evil day came upon us. Your forefathers crossed the great waters and landed upon this island. Their numbers were small. They found friends and not enemies. They told us they had fled from their own country for fear of wicked men, and had come here to enjoy their religion. They asked for a small seat. We took pity on them, granted their request, and they sat down amongst us. We gave them corn and meat. They gave us poison [rum] in return.

The white people, brother, had now found our country. Tidings were carried back and more came amongst us. Yet we did not fear them. We took them to be friends. They called us brothers. We believed them and gave them a larger seat. At length their numbers greatly increased. They wanted more land. They wanted our country. Our eyes were opened, and our minds became uneasy. Wars took place. Indians were hired to fight against Indians, and many of our people were destroyed.

Brother, our seats were once large, and yours were very small. You have now become a great people, and we have scarcely a place left to spread our blankets. You have got our country, but you are not satisfied.

Red Jacket, Seneca (Iroquois)

DID I NOT TELL YOU the last time we met that whilst Red Jacket lived you would get no more land of the Indians? How, then, while you see him alive and strong, do you think to make him a liar?

Red Jacket, Seneca (Iroquois)

THE INDIAN WARRIOR

THE GREAT SPIRIT MADE US, the Indians, and gave us this land we live in. He gave us the buffalo, the antelope, and the deer for food and clothing. . . . We fought our enemies and feasted our friends. Our braves drove away all who would take our game. . . . Our children were many and our herds were large. Our old men talked with spirits and made good medicine. Our young men herded the horses and made love to the girls. Where the tipi was, there we stayed and no house imprisoned us. No one said, "To this line is my land, to that is yours." In this way our fathers lived and were happy. . . . I shall soon lie down to rise no more. While my spirit is with my body the smoke of my breath shall be towards the Sun for he knows all things and knows that I am still true to him.

Red Cloud, Sioux

WHEN THE WHITE MAN treats an Indian as they treat each other, then we will have no more wars. We shall all be alike—brothers of one father and one mother, with one sky above us and one government for all. Then the Great Spirit Chief who rules above will smile upon this land, and send rain to wash out the bloody spots made by brothers' hands from the face of the earth. For this time the Indian race are waiting and praying. I hope that no more groans of wounded men and women will ever go to the ear of the Great Spirit Chief above, and that all people may be one people.

Chief Joseph (Rolling Thunder), Nez Perce

WE THEN MARCHED on to the Yellowstone Basin. On the way, we captured one white man and two white women. We released them at the end of three days. They were treated kindly. The women were not insulted. Can the white soldiers tell me of one time when Indian women were taken prisoners and held three days, and then released without being insulted?

Chief Joseph (Rolling Thunder), Nez Perce

Red Cloud, Sioux, 1880

Sitting Bull, Sioux,
c. 1883

THE INDIAN WARRIOR

WHY WILL YOU TAKE by force what you may have quietly by love? Why will you destroy us who supply you with food? What can you get by war? We can hide our provisions and run into the woods; then you will starve for wronging your friends. Why are you jealous of us? We are unarmed, and willing to give you what you ask, if you come in a friendly manner, and not with swords and guns, as if to make war upon an enemy. I am not so simple as not to know that it is much better to eat good meat, sleep comfortably, live quietly with my wives and children, laugh and be merry with the English, and trade for their copper and hatchets, than to run away from them, and to lie cold in the woods, feed on acorns, roots and . . . be so hunted that I can neither eat nor sleep. . . . So I must end my miserable life. Take away your guns and swords, the cause of all our jealousy, or you may all die in the same manner.

Wahunsonacock, Powhatan

WHAT TREATY THAT the whites have kept has the red man broken? Not one. What treaty that the whites ever made with us red men have they kept? Not one. When I was a boy the Sioux owned the world. The sun rose and set on their land. They sent ten thousand horsemen to battle. Where are the warriors today? Who slew them? Where are our lands? Who owns them? What white man can say I ever stole his lands or a penny of his money? Yet they say I am a thief. What white woman, however lonely, was ever when a captive insulted by me? Yet they say I am a bad Indian. What white man has ever seen me drunk? Who has ever come to me hungry and gone unfed? Who has ever seen me beat my wives or abuse my children? What law have I broken? Is it wrong for me to love my own? Is it wicked in me because my skin is red; because I am a Sioux; because I was born where my father lived; because I would die for my people and my country?

Sitting Bull, Sioux

THE INDIAN WARRIOR

I APPEAL TO ANY WHITE MAN to say, if ever he entered Logan's cabin hungry, and he gave him not meat; if ever he came cold and naked, and he clothed him not. During the course of the last long and bloody war, Logan remained idle in his cabin, an advocate for peace. Such was my love for the whites, that my countrymen pointed as they passed, and said, "Logan is the friend of white men." I had even thought to have lived with you, but for the injuries of one man. Col. Cresap, the last spring, in cold blood, and unprovoked, murdered all the relations of Logan, not sparing even my women and children. There runs not a drop of my blood in the veins of any living creature. This called on me for revenge. I have sought it; I have killed many; I have fully glutted my vengeance. For my country I rejoice at the beams of peace; but do not harbor a thought that mine is the joy of fear. Logan never felt fear. He will not turn on his heel to save his life. Who is there to mourn for Logan? Not one.

Logan, Cayuga (Iroquois)

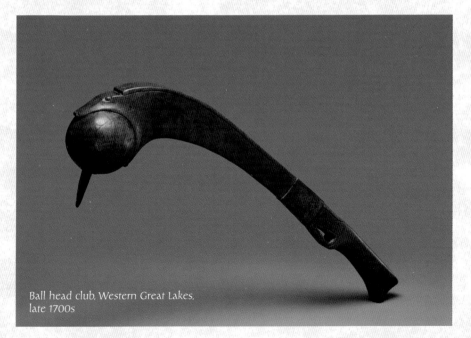

Ball head club, Western Great Lakes, late 1700s

THE INDIAN WARRIOR

Ball head clubs, Lenape,
Delaware Valley, c. 1650

ACCURSED BE THE RACE that has seized on our country and made women
of our warriors. Our fathers, from their tombs, reproach us as slaves
and cowards. I hear them now in the wailing winds. The Muscogee was
once a mighty people. The Georgians trembled at your war-whoop, and
the maidens of my tribe, on the distant lakes, sung the prowess of your
warriors and sighed for their embraces. Now your very blood is white;
your tomahawks have no edge; your bows and arrows were buried with
your fathers. Oh! Muscogees, brethren of my mother, brush from your
eyelids the sleep of slavery; once more strike for vengeance — once more
for your country. The spirits of the mighty dead complain. Their tears drop
from the weeping skies. Let the white race perish. They seize your land;
they corrupt your women; they trample on the ashes of your dead! Back,
whence they came, upon a trail of blood, they must be driven.

Tecumseh, Shawnee

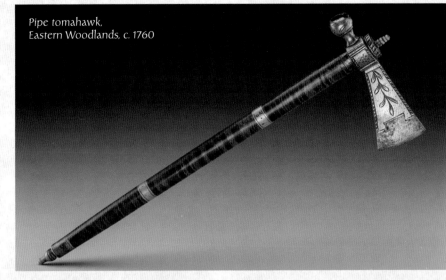

Pipe tomahawk,
Eastern Woodlands, c. 1760

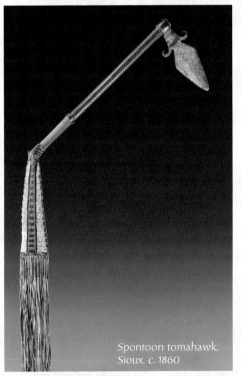

Spontoon tomahawk,
Sioux, c. 1860

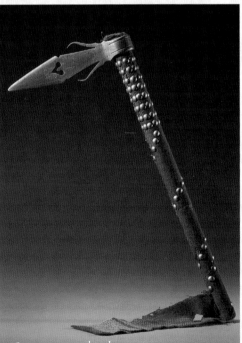

Spontoon tomahawk,
Crow, mid to late 1800s

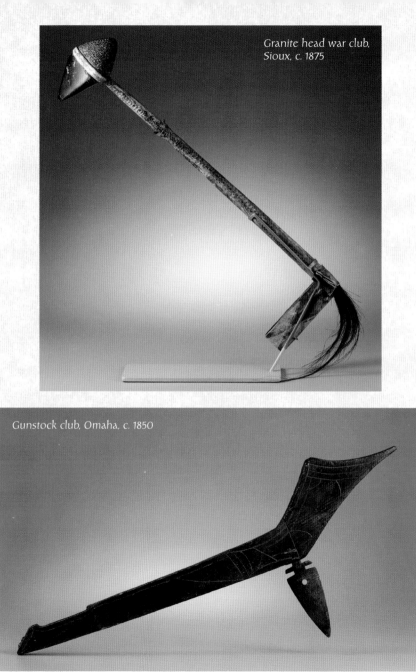

Granite head war club,
Sioux, c. 1875

Gunstock club, Omaha, c. 1850

THE INDIAN WARRIOR

I AM TIRED OF FIGHTING. . . . My people, some of them, have run
away to the hills, and have no blankets, no food. No one knows
where they are—perhaps freezing to death. I want to have time
to look for my children, and see how many of them I can find.
Maybe I shall find them among the dead. Hear me, my chiefs! I am
tired; my heart is sick and sad. From where the sun now stands, I
will fight no more forever.

Chief Joseph (Rolling Thunder), Nez Perce

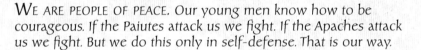

WE ARE PEOPLE OF PEACE. Our young men know how to be
courageous. If the Paiutes attack us we fight. If the Apaches attack
us we fight. But we do this only in self-defense. That is our way.

Unidentified Hopi

MY HEART IS A STONE: heavy with the sadness for my people;
cold with the knowledge that no treaty will keep whites out of
our lands; hard with the determination to resist as long as I live
and breathe. Now we are weak and many of our people are
afraid. But hear me: a single twig breaks, but the bundle of twigs is
strong. Someday I will embrace our brother tribes and draw them
into a bundle and together we will win our country back from the
whites.

Tecumseh, Shawnee

THE INDIAN WARRIOR

Kachina doll, Hopi,
early 1900s

Counting coup,
by unknown Cheyenne

CERTAINLY THEY ARE A HEARTLESS NATION. They have made some of their
people servants—yes, slaves! We have never believed in keeping slaves,
but it seems that these whites do! The greatest object of their lives seems
to be to acquire possessions—to be rich. They desire to possess the whole
world. . . . They are a wonderful people. They have divided the day into
hours, like the moons of the year. In fact, they measure everything. Not
one of them would let so much as a turnip go from his field unless he
received full value for it. I understand that their great men make a feast
and invite many, but when the feast is over the guests are required to
pay for what they have eaten before leaving the house. . . . I am also
informed, but this I hardly believe, that their Great Chief [President]
compels every man to pay him for the land he lives upon and all his
personal goods—even for his own existence—every year! I am sure we
could not live under such a law. In war they have leaders and war-chiefs
of different grades. The common warriors are driven forward like a herd
of antelopes to face the foe. It is on account of this manner of fighting—
from compulsion and not from personal bravery—that we count no coup
on them.

White Footprint, Sioux

THE INDIAN WARRIOR

ALL OF THE BEST CLOTHING was taken along with him when any warrior set out upon a search for conflict. If a battle seemed about to occur, the warrior's first important preparatory act was to jerk off all his ordinary clothing. He then hurriedly got out his fine garments. If he had time to do so he rebraided his hair, painted his face in his own particular way, did everything needful to prepare himself for presenting the most splendid personal appearance. That is, he got himself ready to die. The idea of full dress in preparation for a battle comes not from a belief that it will add to the fighting ability. The preparation is for death, in case that should be the result of the conflict. Every Indian wants to look his best when he goes to meet the Great Spirit. . . .

The naked fighters, among the Cheyennes and Sioux, were such warriors as specially fortified themselves by prayer and other devotional exercises. They had special instruction from medicine men. Their naked bodies were painted in peculiar ways, each according to the direction of his favorite spiritual guide, and each had ' medicine charm given to him by this guide. A warrior thus m. ready for battle was supposed to be proof against the weapor enemy. He placed himself in the forefront of the attack or the a His thought was: "I am so protected by my medicine that I do no need to dress for death. No bullet nor arrow can harm me now."

Wooden Leg, Cheyenne

+ +
+ +

A WARRIOR WHO HAD MORE than he needed would make a feast. He went around and invited the old and needy. . . . The man who could thank the food—some worthy old medicine man or warrior—said ". . . look to the old, they are worthy of old age; they have seen their days and proven themselves. With the help of the Great Spirit, they have attained a ripe old age. At this age the old can predict or give knowledge or wisdom, whatever it is; it is so. . . ."

Black Elk, Sioux

THE INDIAN WARRIOR

WHEN A CHILD my mother taught me the legends of our people; taught me of the sun and sky, the moon and stars, the clouds and storms. She also taught me to kneel and pray to Usen for strength, health, wisdom, and protection. We never prayed against any person, but if we had aught against any individual we ourselves took vengeance. We were taught that Usen does not care for the petty quarrels of men.

Geronimo, Apache

LOOK NOW, MY BROTHER, the white people think we have no brains in our heads; but that they are great and big, and that makes them make war with us: we are but a little handful to what you are; but remember, when you look for a wild turkey you cannot always find it, it is so little it hides itself under the bushes: and when you hunt for a rattlesnake, you cannot find it; and perhaps it will bite you before you see it.

Shingis, Lenape

THIS WAR DID NOT SPRING UP here on our land; this war was brought upon us by the children of the Great Father who came to take our land from us without price, and who, in our land, do a great many evil things. . . . It has been our wish to live here in our country peaceably, . . . but the Great Father has filled it with soldiers who think only of our death. Some of our people who have gone from here in order that they should have a change, and others who have gone north to hunt, have been attacked by soldiers from this direction, and when they have got north have been attacked by soldiers from the other side, and now when they are willing to come back the soldiers stand between them to keep them from coming home. It seems to me that there is a better way than this. When people come to trouble, it is better for both parties to come together without arms and talk it over and find some peaceful way to settle it.

Spotted Tail, Sioux

Spotted Tail, Sioux,
c. 1880

Sintégaléska. Spotted Tail.   Oglala Dakota. 1.

THE INDIAN WARRIOR

Choctaw Eagle Dance,
by George Catlin, c. 1845

BROTHER: WHEN YOU were young we were strong; we fought by your
side; but our arms are now broken. You have grown large. My people have
become small.

Brother: My voice is weak; you can scarcely hear me; it is not the
shout of a warrior, but the wail of an infant. I have lost it in mourning over
the misfortunes of my people. These are their graves, and in those aged
pines you hear the ghosts of the departed. Their ashes are here, and we
have been left to protect them. Our warriors are nearly all gone to the far
country west; but here are our dead. Shall we go, too, and give their bones
to the wolves?

Brother: Two sleeps have passed since we heard your talk. We have
thought upon it. You ask us to leave our country, and tell us it is our Father's
wish. We would not desire to displease our Father. We respect him, and you
his child. But the Choctaw always thinks. We want time to answer.

THE INDIAN WARRIOR

Brother: Our hearts are full. Twelve winters ago our chiefs sold our country. Every warrior that you see here was opposed to the treaty. If the dead could have been counted, it could never have been made; but alas! Their tears came in the rain-drops, and their voices in the wailing wind, but the pale faces knew it not, and our land was taken away.

Brother: We do not now complain. The Choctaw suffers, but he never weeps. You have the strong arm, and we cannot resist. But the pale face worships the Great Spirit. So does the red man. The Great Spirit loves truth. When you took our country, you promised us land. There is your promise in the book. Twelve times have the trees dropped their leaves, and yet we have received no land. Our houses have been taken from us. The white man's plough turns up the bones of our fathers. We dare not kindle our fires; and yet you said we might remain and you would give us land. Brother: Is this truth?

Colonel Cobb, Choctaw

Choctaw Village,
by François Bernard, 1869

THE INDIAN WARRIOR

FATHER, THE VOICE of the Seneca nation speaks to you the great Councilor, in whose heart, the wise men of the thirteen fires have placed their wisdom. It may be very small in your ears, and we therefore entreat you to hearken with attention. For we are about to speak of things which are to us very great. When your army entered the Country of the Six Nations, we called you the town-destroyer and to this day, when that name is heard, our women look behind them and turn pale, and our children cling close to the neck of their mothers. Our councilors and warriors are men, and can not be afraid; but their hearts are grieved with the fears of our women and children, and desire that it may be buried so deep as to be heard no more. When you gave us peace we called you father, because you promised to secure us in the possession of our land. . . .

Father, your commissioners when they drew the line which separated the land then given up to you, from that which you agreed should remain to be ours did, most solemnly promise, that we should be secured in the peaceable possession of the lands which we inhabited, East and North, of that line. Does this promise bind you? Father, you have said we were in your hand, and that by closing it, you could crush us to nothing; are you determined to crush us? If you are, tell us so that those of our nation who have become your children and are determined to die so, may know what to do: In this case one chief has said he would ask you to put him out of pain: Another, who will not think of dying by the hand of his father, has said he will retire to the Chataughque, eat of the faral root, and sleep with his fathers in peace. Before you determine on a measure so unjust, look up to the God who made us, as well as you; we hope He will not permit you to destroy the whole of our nation.

Cornplanter, Seneca (Iroquois)

Cornplanter, Seneca,
by Frederick Bartoli, 1796

Black Hawk. Sauk.
by George Catlin. 1832

THE INDIAN WARRIOR

THE PATH TO GLORY is rough, and many gloomy hours obscure it. May the Great Spirit shed light on yours—and that you may never experience the humility that the power of the American Government has reduced me to, is the wish of him, who, in his native forests, was once as proud and bold as yourself.

Black Hawk, Sauk

+ +
+ +

YOU HAVE TAKEN ME PRISONER with all my warriors. I am much grieved, for I expected, if I did not defeat you, to hold out much longer, and give you more trouble before I surrendered. I tried hard to bring you into ambush, but your last general understands Indian fighting. The first one was not so wise. When I saw that I could not beat you by Indian fighting, I determined to rush on you, and fight you face to face. I fought hard. But your guns were well aimed. The bullets flew like birds in the air, and whizzed by our ears like the wind through the trees in the winter. My warriors fell around me; it began to look dismal. I saw my evil day at hand. The sun rose dim on us in the morning, and at night it sunk in a dark cloud, and looked like a ball of fire.

That was the last sun that shone on Black Hawk. His heart is dead, and no longer beats quick in his bosom. He is now a prisoner to the white men; they will do with him as they wish. But he can stand torture, and is not afraid of death. He is no coward. Black Hawk is an Indian.

Black Hawk, Sauk

THE INDIAN WARRIOR

My PEOPLE HAVE NEVER first drawn a bow or fired a gun against the whites. There has been trouble on the line between us and my young men have danced the war dance. But it was not begun by us. It was you to send the first soldier and we who sent out the second. Two years ago I came upon this road, following the buffalo, that my wives and children might have their cheeks plump and their bodies warm. But the soldiers fired on us, and since that time there has been a noise like that of a thunderstorm and we have not known which way to go. . . . The blue dressed soldiers and the Utes came from out of the night when it was dark and still, and for camp fires they lit our lodges. Instead of hunting game they killed my braves. . . . So it was in Texas. They made sorrow come in our camps, and we went out like the buffalo bulls when the cows are attacked. When we found them, we killed them, and their scalps hang in our lodges. The Comanches are not weak and blind, like the pups of a dog when seven sleeps old. They are strong and farsighted, like grown horses. . . . But there are things which you have said which I do not like. They were not sweet like sugar but bitter like gourds. You said that you wanted

THE INDIAN WARRIOR

War flag, Plains, 1800s

to put us upon a reservation, to build our houses and make us medicine lodges. I do not want them. I was born on the prairie where the wind blew free and there was nothing to break the light of the sun. I was born where there were no enclosures and where everything drew a free breath. I want to die there and not within walls. I know every stream and every wood between the Rio Grande and the Arkansas. I have hunted and lived over the country. I lived like my fathers before me, and like them, I lived happily. . . . If the Texans had kept out of my country there might have been peace. But that which you now say we must live on is too small. The Texans have taken away the places where the grass grew the thickest and the timber was the best. Had we kept that we might have done the things you ask. But it is too late. The white man has the country which we loved, and we only wish to wander on the prairie until we die. . . . I want it all clear and pure and I wish it so that all who go through among my people may find peace when they come in and leave it when they go out.

Ten Bears, Comanche

THE INDIAN WARRIOR

Crow warriors, c. 1908

THE INDIAN WARRIOR

WHENEVER THERE IS any trouble,
I shall not die but get through.
Though arrows are many, I shall arrive.
My heart is manly.

Crow Song

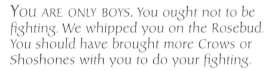

I AM SPOTTED HORSE, chief of the Crows.
This is a nice day to die, and I am going
but not alone. I take one of you with me.

Spotted Horse, Crow

YOU ARE ONLY BOYS. You ought not to be
fighting. We whipped you on the Rosebud.
You should have brought more Crows or
Shoshones with you to do your fighting.

Wooden Leg, Cheyenne, addressed to
General George Armstrong Custer's
Seventh Cavalry

ETERNAL ARE THE HEAVENS and the earth;
Old people are poorly off.
Do not be afraid.

Crow Song

Battle of the Little Bighorn,
by Amos Bad Heart Bull,
Sioux, late 1880s or early 1900s

THE INDIAN WARRIOR

SOMETIMES DURING THE NIGHT or stillness of day, a voice would be heard singing the brave song. This meant that sorrow was present— either a brave was going on the warpath and expected to die, or else a family was looking for the death of some member of it. The brave song was to fortify one to meet any ordeal bravely and to keep up faltering spirits. I remember, when we children were on our way to Carlisle School, thinking that we were on our way to meet death at the hands of the white people, the older boys sang brave songs, so that we would all meet death according to the code of the Lakota fearlessly.

Standing Bear, Sioux

WAKONDA, YOU SEE ME a poor man. Have pity on me. I go to war to revenge the death of my brother. . . . I have sacrificed, I have smoked, my heart is low, have pity upon me. Give me the bows and arrows of my enemies. Give me their guns. Give me their horses. Give me their bodies. Let me have my face blackened on my return. Let good weather come that I can see. Good dreams give that I can judge where they are. I have suffered. I wish to live. I wish to be revenged. I am poor. I want horses. I will sacrifice. I will smoke. I will remember. Have pity on me.

Unidentified Assiniboine

BEHOLD, I GO FORTH to move around the earth,
Behold, I go forth to move around the earth,
I go forth as the puma that is great in courage.
To move onward I go forth,
I go forth as the puma that is great in courage.
Behold, I go forth to move around the earth.

Osage Warrior's Song from the Mourning Rite

Wets It, Assiniboine,
c. 1898

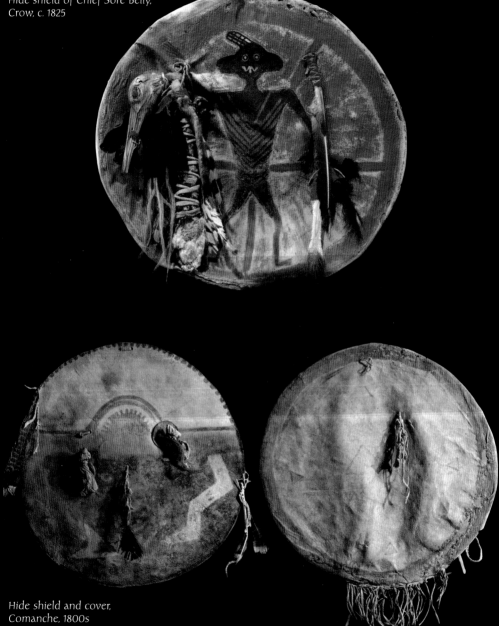

Hide shield of Chief Sore Belly,
Crow, c. 1825

Hide shield and cover,
Comanche, 1800s

Hide shield,
Pueblo, 1800s

Prehistoric petroglyphs,
including figures identified
by Zuni as twin gods of war.
Galisteo Basin, New Mexico

THE INDIAN WARRIOR

Is THERE ANYONE WHO
Would weep for me?
My wife
Would weep for me.

Winnebago Song

THEY BROUGHT THE ONES who had been killed by the white
people. My aunts were with me. My mother, my father, my aunts,
held me and went with me. I came there; I was pregnant. They
would not let me see him, my husband. Only my mother saw
him. She told me. It was not good. . . . So they buried them in
the graveyard, just before sunset. . . . If one's husband dies one
will not sleep. She will lie down as if she sleeps, and when sleep
overcomes her she will sleep. But after a little while she will wake,
and will not sleep. She will cry, she will be lonely. She will not care
to eat. She will take thought of what to do and where to go.
When a child or a relative dies, one cries for them properly.
Husband and wife talk together to relieve their thoughts. Then
they will forget their trouble. But when one's husband dies there
is no happiness. . . .

    For one year I would cry. I was thoughtful for my old husband.
Then father spoke with me. Then I was happy. I did not worry. My
uncle desired it for me. "It is all right, niece. Do not cry. It cannot be
helped. It is ever thus. Do not think of where you have come from,
but rather look forward to where you are to go."

Unidentified Zuni

THE INDIAN WARRIOR

I WAS A YOUNG MAN when I promised myself to be a peaceful person. My soul said to me in a dream: *"I shall never kill anyone; but in self-defense I will fight it out to the finish."*

Unidentified Paiute

THE WHITE MEN were many and we could not hold our own with them. We were like deer. They were like grizzly bears. We had a small country. Their country was large. We were contented to let things remain as the Great Spirit had made them. They were not, and would change the rivers if they did not suit them.

Chief Joseph (Rolling Thunder), Nez Perce

WE DO NOT BREAK TREATIES. We make but few contracts, and them we remember well. The whites make so many that they are liable to forget them. The white chief seems not able to govern his braves. The Great Father seems powerless in the face of his children. He sometimes becomes angry when he sees the wrongs of his people committed on the red man, and his voice becomes loud as the roaring winds. But like the wind it soon dies away and leaves the sullen calm of unheeded oppression. We hope now that a better time has come.

Sitting Bear (Satank), Kiowa

Treaty of Fort Stanwix,
signed 1768

Unidentified Cheyenne, carrying a scalp

THE INDIAN WARRIOR

WELL, A WAR PARTY
Which was supposed to come
Now is here
I have obliterated every trace of them.

Sioux Song

NOW, MY SON, if you do not obtain a spirit to strengthen you, you
will not amount to anything in the estimation of your fellow men.
They will show you little respect. Perhaps they will make fun of you.
Do not die in the village. It is not good to die there. Whenever a
person is grown up that is what is told him. Nor is it good, my son
to let women journey ahead of you from amidst the village. "It is not
good thus to let women die before you." . . . Especially difficult is it
to be leader on the warpath. So they say. If you do not become an
individual warranted to lead a war party, yet mistaking yourself for
one although really an ordinary warrior, you "throw away a man,"
your act will be considered most disgraceful. A mourner might harm
you in revenge for the fact that you have caused him to mourn, and
burn you with embers. Your people will all be sad, both on account of
your disgrace and on account of the pain inflicted upon you.
  My son, not with the blessing of one of the spirits merely, nor
with the blessing of twenty, for that matter, can you go on the
warpath. You must have the blessing of all the spirits above the
earth, and of all those on the earth, and of all those who are pierced
through the earth; of all those under the earth; of all those who are
under the water; of all those that are on the sides of the earth, i.e.,
all the four winds; of the Disease-giver; of the Sun; of the Daylight;
of the Moon; of the Earth; and of all those who are in control of war
powers — with the blessings of all these deities must you be provided
before you can lead a successful war party.

Unidentified Winnebago

Tecumseh, Shawnee, colorized version of Benson Lossing's engraving, based on a sketch by Pierre Le Dru, c. 1808

Brothers, when the white men first set foot on our grounds, they were hungry; they had no place on which to spread their blankets, or to kindle their fires. They were feeble; they could do nothing for themselves. Our fathers commiserated their distress, and shared freely with them whatever the Great Spirit had given his red children. They gave them food when hungry, medicine when sick, spread skins for them to sleep on, and gave them grounds, that they might hunt and raise corn. Brothers, the white people are like poisonous serpents: when chilled, they are feeble and harmless; but invigorate them with warmth, and they sting their benefactors to death. The white people came among us feeble; and now that we have made them strong, they wish to kill us, or drive us back, as they would wolves and panthers. Brothers, the white men are not friends to the Indians: at first, they only asked for land sufficient for a wigwam; now, nothing will satisfy them but the whole of our hunting grounds, from the rising to the setting sun. . . . Brothers, my people wish for peace; the red men all wish for peace; but where the white people are, there

44

is no peace for them, except it be on the bosom of our mother. . . . The red men have borne many and great injuries; they ought to suffer them no longer. My people will not; they are determined on vengeance; they have taken up the tomahawk; they will make it fat with blood; they will drink the blood of the white people. Brothers, my people are brave and numerous; but the white people are too strong for them alone. I wish you to take up the tomahawk with them. If we all unite, we will cause the rivers to stain the great waters with their blood. . . . Brothers, the white people send runners amongst us; they wish to make us enemies, that they may sweep over and desolate our hunting grounds, like devastating winds, or rushing waters. . . . Brothers, we must be united; we must smoke the same pipe; we must fight each other's battles; and, more than all, we must love the Great Spirit: he is for us; he will destroy our enemies, and make all his red children happy.

Tecumseh, Shawnee

THE INDIAN WARRIOR

AT THE BEGINNING of the attack [of the soldiers], Black Kettle, with his wife and White Antelope, took their position before Black Kettle's lodge and remained there after all others had left the camp. At last Black Kettle, seeing that it was useless to stay longer, started to run, calling out to White Antelope to follow him, but White Antelope refused and stood there ready to die, with arms folded, singing his death song: "Nothing lives long, except the earth and the mountains," until he was shot down by the soldiers.

George Bent, Cheyenne

+
+┼+
+

"CAN YOU WALK ACROSS?" I asked him. "No," he said. "I can go no farther. I am finished. Leave me and run." He sank down at my feet, and Goes-against-the-enemy, who had already crossed the creek, came back. "Sit down beside me," whispered Big-horn, "and sing with me while I go to my Father." We sat down and sang there in the rain. And he sang with us until his heart was still. Big-horn, my friend, was dead in the enemy's country. My heart was on the ground beside him. We gave him the best things we had, my necklace of bear's teeth and Goes-against-the-enemy's belt of porcupine quills, that he might offer them to our Father, and we left him lying on a bed we made in the dark. But we carefully covered him with willows so that the Flatheads should not find him, nor the wolves disturb his body. "When we come back to get him, if we live to come," I said to Goes-against-the-enemy, "we will sing of his deeds and ask his spirit to stay always with us, as we stayed with him when he was here." "Yes," he answered, "we will do as you say, and now let us make our hearts sing because our friend died unafraid."

Plenty Coups, Crow

Plenty Coups, Crow, 1880

Plains war shirt,
mid to late 1800s

Above: Rod-armor vest, Aleut, late 1800s

Left: Unidentified Karuk with rod-armor vest, 1898

Bear claw necklace, Sioux or Meskwaki, c. 1825

Kno-Shr, Kansa, 1853

THE INDIAN WARRIOR

Pawnee scouts with interpreter,
c. 1870

THE INDIAN WARRIOR

You MUST TRUST always in Tirawa. He made us, and through Him we live. When you grow up, you must be a man. Be brave, and face whatever danger may meet you. Do not forget, when you look back to your young days, that I have raised you, and always supported you. You had no father to do it. Your father was a chief, but you must not think of that. Because he was a chief, it does not follow that you will be one. It is not the man who stays in the lodge that becomes great; it is the man who works, who sweats, who is always tired from going on the warpath. . . . When you get to be a man, remember that it is his ambition that makes the man. If you go on the warpath, do not turn around when you have gone part way, but go on as far as you were going, and then come back. If I should live to see you become a man, I want you to become a great man. I want you to think about the hard times we have been through.

Take pity on people who are poor, because we have been poor, and people have taken pity on us. If I live to see you a man, and to go off on the warpath, I would not cry if I were to hear that you had been killed in battle. That is what makes a man: to fight and to be brave. I should be sorry to see you die from sickness. If you are killed, I would rather have you die in the open air, so that the birds of the air will eat your flesh, and the wind will breathe on you and blow over your bones. It is better to be killed in the open air than to be smothered in the earth. Love your friend and never desert him. If you see him surrounded by the enemy, do not run away. Go to him, and if you cannot save him, be killed together, and let your bones lie side by side. Be killed on a hill; high up. Your grandfather said it is not manly to be killed in a hollow. It is not a man who is talking to you, advising you. Heed my words, even if I am a woman.

Mother of Lone Chief, Pawnee

THE INDIAN WARRIOR

CROW INDIANS
You must watch your horses
A horse thief
Often
I am.

Sioux Song

[A]s WE WERE GOING along the side of a foothill, I saw four Crow warriors coming toward us. I said to the young men: "Come near and stand by me. Four warriors are coming." The young men said, "Let us run and hide." I said: "Wakan Tanka has but one path. No matter how or where you die you must go by that path. Let us stand together and fight." I had a gun and two revolvers, one of the young men had a quiver of arrows, and the other had a double-barreled gun. I sang my death song for I felt sure that I was soon to die. . . . There was an immense rock in front of us, and in a crack of the rock grew a cherry tree. It was through this crack that I watched the warriors. One had his hair combed high and carried a gun; the others had bows and arrows, and as they came nearer I saw that one of them was only a boy. I said to my companions: "Now work and be brave. We have only three to fight, as one of them is a boy."

When they came opposite the crack in the rock I fired, but my gun snapped and did not go off. . . . The man with the gun saw me and aimed at me, but I grabbed his arm so he could not fire. My companions chased the others, and I fought hand to hand with the man for an hour. Then I called my companions; they succeeded in taking the gun from the man, and I had the satisfaction of killing him. The boy ran away, but my companions brought back the two Crows, whom they had taken captive. One of them said: "We are Crow Indians. We want to live. We give you our bodies, and we give you the right to wear the feathers, only let us go." So we gave them back their lives. Because of that act I was appointed a chief, for it was considered a brave deed to spare the lives of two enemies.

Red Fox, Sioux

Red Fox, Sioux, 1889

THE INDIAN WARRIOR

[T]HE GOOD THINGS which men do are often
buried in the ground and forgot, while their
evil deeds are stripped naked and proclaimed
to the world. My father—when I came it was
simply to hear what you had to say to me. I
little thought I should have to defend myself. If
I had been your enemy I would doubtless have
taken some caution. . . . As to what has or may
be done in council here, I have nothing to say.
It is simply to repeat what I said to my great
father, the president of the United States. You
heard it, and no doubt remember it. It is simply
to say, that my lands can never be surrendered.
I was cheated, basely cheated, in the contract.
While I live they shall never be surrendered.

My father—I call heaven and earth to
witness, and smoke the pipe in evidence of
the truth and sincerity of what I have said.
I remember the sentiments my great father
expressed towards me. I hope he and you still
cherish the same. If you do, I know you will
receive the pipe. My only desire is to smoke
it with you—to grasp your sacred hand, and
claim the protection of the United States for
myself and tribe. I hope as the pipe touches
your lips, it will operate as a blessing on all
my tribe—that the smoke will rise like a cloud,
and as it passes away will carry with it all the
animosities that have arisen between us.

Black Thunder, Meskwaki

THE INDIAN WARRIOR

Sauk and Meskwaki Warriors,
by Karl Bodmer, 1833

Coacoochee, Seminole,
by Nathaniel Orr, 1848

HAS NOT COACOOCHEE . . . sat with you by the council-fire at
midnight, when the wolf and white man were around us? Have
I not led the war dance, and sung the song of the Seminole? Did
not the spirits of our mothers, our wives, and our children stand
around us? Has not my scalping-knife been red with blood, and
the scalps of our enemy been drying in our camps? . . .

If Coacoochee is to die, he can die like a man. It is not my
heart that shakes; no, it never trembles; but I feel for those now in
the woods, pursued night and day by the soldiers; for those who
fought with us, until we were weak. The sun shines bright today,
the day is clear; so let your hearts be: the Great Spirit will guide
you.

At night, when you camp, take these pipes and tobacco, build
a fire when the moon is up and bright, dance around it, then let
the fire go out, and just before the break of day, when the deer

THE INDIAN WARRIOR

sleeps, and the moon whispers to the dead, you will hear the voices of those who have gone to the Great Spirit; they will give you strong hearts and head to carry the talk of Coacoochee.

Say to my band that my feet are chained. I cannot walk, yet I send them my word as true from the heart, as if I was on the warpath or in the deer-hunt. I am not a boy; Coacoochee can die, not with a shivering hand, but as when grasping the rifle with my warriors around me. . . .

The great white chief (Po-car-ger) will be kind to us. He says, when my band comes in I shall again walk my land free, with my band around me. He has given you forty days to do this business in. . . . Take these sticks; here are thirty-nine, one for each day; this, much larger than the rest, with blood upon it, is the fortieth. When the others are thrown away, and this only remains, say to my people, that with the setting sun Coacoochee hangs like a dog, with none but the white men to hear his last words.

Come then; come by the stars, as I have led you to battle! Come, for the voice of Coacoochee speaks to you!

Coacoochee (Wildcat), Seminole (Miccosukee)

Attack of the Seminoles on U.S. Army blockhouse, by T.F. Gray and James, 1837

THE INDIAN WARRIOR

Little Crow, Sioux, 1858

THE INDIAN WARRIOR

TA-Ó-YA-TE-DÚ-TA IS NOT A COWARD, and he is not a fool! When did he run away from his enemies? When did he leave his braves behind him on the warpath and turn back to his tipi? When he ran away from your enemies, he walked behind on your trail with his face to the Ojibways and covered your backs as a she-bear covers her cubs! Is Ta-ó-ya-te-dú-ta without scalps? Look at his war feathers! Behold the scalp locks of your enemies hanging there on his lodgepoles! Do they call him a coward? Ta-ó-ya-te-dú-ta is not a coward, and he is not a fool. Braves, you are like little children: you know not what you are doing. You are full of the white man's devil water. You are like dogs in the Hot Moon when they run mad and snap at their own shadows. We are only little herds of buffalo left scattered; the great herds that once covered the prairies are no more.

See! — the white men are like the locusts when they fly so thick that the whole sky is a snowstorm. You may kill one — two — ten; yes, as many as the leaves in the forest yonder, and their brothers will not miss them. Kill one — two — ten, and ten times ten will come to kill you. Count your fingers all day long and white men with guns in their hands will come faster than you can count. Yes; they fight among themselves — away off. Do you hear the thunder of their big guns? No; it would take you two moons to run down to where they are fighting, and all the way your path would be among white soldiers as thick as tamaracks in the swamps of the Ojibways. Yes; they fight among themselves, but if you strike at them they will all turn on you and devour you and your women and little children just as the locusts in their time fall on the trees and devour all the leaves in one day.

You are fools. You cannot see the face of your chief; your eyes are full of smoke. You cannot hear his voice; your ears are full of roaring waters. Braves, you are little children — you are fools. You will die like the rabbits when the hungry wolves hunt them in the Hard Moon. Ta-ó-ya-te-dú-ta is not a coward; he will die with you.

Little Crow (Ta-ó-ya-te-dú-ta), Sioux

THE INDIAN WARRIOR

WHEN THE WHITE MAN first came to these shores, the Muscogees gave him land and kindled him a fire to make him comfortable.... But when the White man had warmed himself before the Indian's fire, and filled himself with the Indian's hominy, he became very large; he stopped not for the mountain tops, and his feet covered the plains and the valleys. His hands grasped the eastern and western sea. Then he became our great father. He loved his red children, but said, "You must move a little farther, lest I should, by accident, tread on you."

With one foot he pushed the red man over the Oconee and with the other he trampled down the graves of his fathers. But our great father still loved his red children, and he soon made them another talk. He said much, but it all meant nothing, but "move a little farther; you are too near me." I have heard a great many talks from our great father, and they all begun and ended the same. Brothers! When he made us a talk on a former occasion, he said, "Get a little farther; go beyond the Oconee and the Oakmulgee; there is a pleasant country." Now he says, "The land you live on is not yours; go beyond the Mississippi; there is game, there you may remain while the grass grows or the water runs." Brothers! Will not our great father come there also? He loves his red children, and his tongue is not forked.

Speckled Snake, Cherokee

IF I HAD KNOWN that I would be sent to the penitentiary I would not have surrendered, but when I had been in the penitentiary three years and they were about to turn me out, I told them they might keep me another year if they wished, and I meant what I said. I did not like the way I had been treated. I surrendered in good faith, knowing that many of the whites were acquainted with me and that I had not been a murderer, or present when a murder had been committed, and if I had killed or wounded a man it had been in fair, open fight.

Big Eagle, Sioux

THE INDIAN WARRIOR

Big Eagle, Sioux, 1864

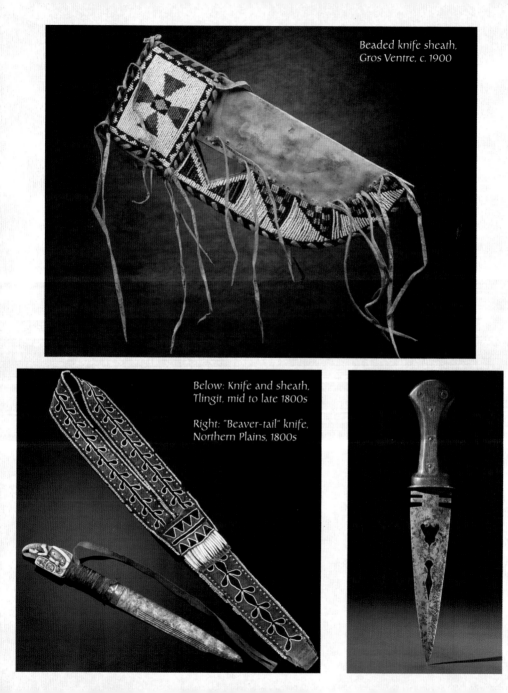

Beaded knife sheath,
Gros Ventre, c. 1900

Below: Knife and sheath,
Tlingit, mid to late 1800s

Right: "Beaver-tail" knife,
Northern Plains, 1800s

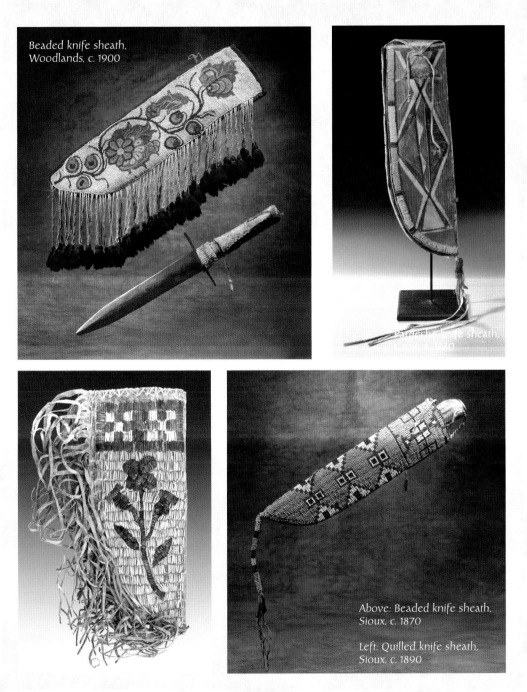

Beaded knife sheath, Woodlands, c. 1900

Quilled knife sheath, c. 1880

Above: Beaded knife sheath, Sioux, c. 1870

Left: Quilled knife sheath, Sioux, c. 1890

Iron Hawk, Sioux, 1899

THE INDIAN WARRIOR

A MAN BY THE NAME of Little Bear rode up to me on a pinto horse, and he had a very pretty saddle blanket. He said: "Take courage, boy! The earth is all that lasts!" So I rode fast with him and the others downstream, and many of us Hunkpapas gathered on the east side of the river at the foot of a gulch that led back up the hill where the second soldier band was. There was a very brave Shyela with us, and I heard someone say: "He is going!" I looked, and it was this Shyela. He had on a spotted war bonnet and a spotted robe made of some animal's skin and this was fastened with a spotted belt. He was going up the hill alone and we all followed part way. There were soldiers along the ridge up there and they were on foot holding their horses. The Shyela rode right close to them in a circle several times and all the soldiers shot at him. Then he rode back to where we had stopped at the head of the gulch. He was saying: "Ah, ah!" Someone said: "Shyela friend, what is the matter?" He began undoing his spotted belt, and when he shook it, bullets dropped out. He was very sacred and the soldiers could not hurt him. He was a fine looking man.

Iron Hawk, Sioux

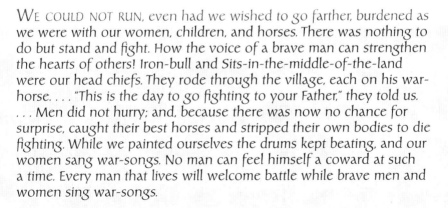

WE COULD NOT RUN, even had we wished to go farther, burdened as we were with our women, children, and horses. There was nothing to do but stand and fight. How the voice of a brave man can strengthen the hearts of others! Iron-bull and Sits-in-the-middle-of-the-land were our head chiefs. They rode through the village, each on his war-horse. . . . "This is the day to go fighting to your Father," they told us. . . . Men did not hurry; and, because there was now no chance for surprise, caught their best horses and stripped their own bodies to die fighting. While we painted ourselves the drums kept beating, and our women sang war-songs. No man can feel himself a coward at such a time. Every man that lives will welcome battle while brave men and women sing war-songs.

Plenty Coups, Crow

THE INDIAN WARRIOR

IT'S ME—I am a war eagle!
The wind is strong, but I am an eagle!
I am not ashamed—no, I am not;
The twisting eagle's quill is on my head.
I see my enemy below me!
I am an eagle, a war eagle!

Iowa Song

LONG HAIR [General Custer] has never returned,
So his woman is crying, crying.
Looking over here, she cries.

Long Hair, horses I had none.
You brought me many. I thank you!
You make me laugh!

Long Hair, guns I had none.
You brought me many. I thank you!
You make me laugh!

Long Hair, where he lies nobody knows.
Crying, they seek him
He lies over here.

Sioux Song

Two Leggings,
Crow, 1908

WE STOPPED TO PUT ON the war shirts, medicines, warbonnets, and leggings we had brought, and painted our faces to show we had been successful. I led six men galloping into camp. When we reached the center of the tipis we circled around, pretending to fight each other. Then we dashed back out, joined the others, and all galloped into camp, five abreast, firing our guns into the air. From the top of a long willow pole I carried my scalp. It was scraped thin, dyed with a mixture of blood and charcoal, and stretched on a willow hop. Everyone was singing; this was my song: "I shall travel to some place. I shall be glad."

Two Leggings, Crow

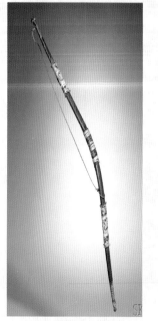

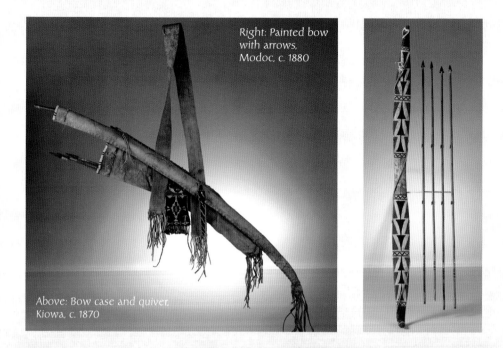

Right: Painted bow with arrows, Modoc, c. 1880

Above: Bow case and quiver, Kiowa, c. 1870

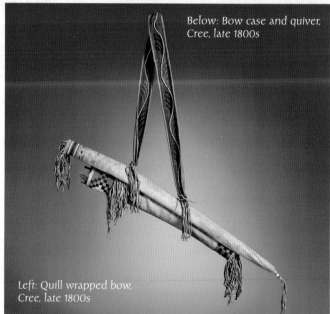

Below: Bow case and quiver, Cree, late 1800s

Left: Quill wrapped bow, Cree, late 1800s

Unidentified Inuit, 1893

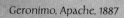
Geronimo, Apache, 1887

THE INDIAN WARRIOR

TO BE ADMITTED AS A WARRIOR a youth must have gone with the warriors of his tribe four separate times on the warpath. . . . On each of these expeditions he acts as servant, cares for the horses, cooks the food, and does whatever duties he should do without being told. He knows what things are to be done, and without waiting to be told is to do them. He is not allowed to speak to any warrior except in answer to questions or when told to speak. During these four wars he is expected to learn the sacred names of everything used in war, for after the tribe enters upon the warpath no common names are used in referring to anything appertaining to war in any way. War is a solemn religious matter.

If, after four expeditions, all the warriors are satisfied that the youth has been industrious, has not spoken out of order, has been discreet in all things, has shown courage in battle, has borne all hardships uncomplainingly, and has exhibited no color of cowardice, or weakness of any kind, he may, by vote of the council, be admitted as a warrior; but if any warrior objects to him upon any account he will be subjected to further tests, and if he meets these courageously, his name may again be proposed.

When he has proven beyond question that he can bear hardships without complaint, and that he is a stranger to fear, he is admitted to the council of the warriors in the lowest rank. After this there is no formal test for promotions, but by common consent he assumes a station on the battlefield, and if that position is maintained with honor, he is allowed to keep it, and may be asked, or may volunteer, to take a higher station, but no warrior would presume to take a higher station unless he had assurance from the leaders of the tribe that his conduct in the first position was worthy of commendation.

Geronimo, Apache

THE INDIAN WARRIOR

WHEN I WAS A YOUNG MAN I went to a medicine-man for advice concerning my future. The medicine-man said: "I have not much to tell you except to help you understand this earth on which you live. If a man is to succeed on the hunt or the warpath, he must not be governed by his inclination, but by an understanding of the ways of animals and of his natural surroundings, gained through close observation. . . ." The medicine-man told me to observe my natural surroundings, and after my talk with him I observed them closely. I watched the changes of the weather, the habits of animals, and all the things by which I might be guided in the future, and I stored this knowledge in my mind.

Lone Man, Sioux

MORE AND MORE we gathered by ourselves to talk and play. Often our talking was of warriors and war, and always in our playing there was the object of training ourselves to become warriors. We had our leaders just as our fathers had, and they became our chiefs in the same manner that men become chiefs, by distinguishing themselves. . . . My people were wise. . . . They never neglected the young or failed to keep before them deeds done by illustrious men of the tribe. Our teachers were willing and thorough. They were our grandfathers, fathers, or uncles. All were quick to praise excellence without speaking a word that might break the spirit of a boy who might be less capable than others. The boy who failed at any lesson got only more lessons, more care, until he was as far as he could go.

Plenty Coups, Crow

THE INDIAN WARRIOR

Unidentified Cheyenne boy, 1907

Moving Robe,
Sioux, c. 1937

THE SOLDIERS BEGAN firing into our camp. Then they ceased firing. I
saw my father preparing to go to the battle. I sang a death song for my
brother who had been killed. My heart was bad. Revenge! Revenge! For
my brother's death. I thought of the death of my young brother, One
Hawk. I ran to a nearby thicket and got my black horse. I painted my face
with crimson and braided my black hair. I was mourning. I was a woman,
but I was not afraid. . . . I am a woman, but I fought for my people.

Moving Robe, Sioux

White Buffalo Woman,
Cheyenne, c. 1907

GREATLY
She
Defending her children
The old woman
Fought for us all.

Winnebago Song

THE INDIAN WARRIOR

ON THE WARPATH
I give place to none
With dauntless courage I live.

Sioux Song

IS IT FOR ME to eat what food I have
And all day sit idle?
Is it for me to drink the sweet water poured out
And all day sit idle?
Is it for me to gaze upon my wife
And all day sit idle?
Is it for me to hold my child in my arms
And all day sit idle?

Papago Song

THE NEXT MORNING, when the village moved, snow was falling
and the air was sharp as a knife. We who had been on the raid
against the Pecunies rode together beside the line of moving
travois, singing our war-songs, while young women smiled at us
and called our names. It was good to live in those days.

Plenty Coups, Crow

Black Elk, Sioux,
late 1880s

MANY OF OUR WARRIORS were following the soldiers up a hill on
the other side of the river. . . . I saw a very pretty young woman
among a band of warriors about to go up to the battle on the hill,
and she was singing like this: "Brothers now your friends have
come! Be brave! Be brave! Would you see me taken captive?"

Black Elk, Sioux

Buffalo Bull, Pawnee,
by George Catlin, 1832

THE INDIAN WARRIOR

NOW HE LIES YONDER.
He who has on a metal shirt.
The protection in which he trusted is set aside.

Pawnee Song

THE SIOUX WOMEN
Pass to and fro wailing
As they gather up
Their wounded men
The voice of their weeping come back to us.

Winnebago Song

AS THE YOUNG MEN
Go by
I was looking for him
It surprises me anew
That he has gone
(It is) something
To which I cannot be reconciled.

Sioux Song

Geronimo and his warriors, Apache, 1886

I WANT TO TALK first of the causes which led me to leave the reservation. . . . I was living peaceably with my family, having plenty to eat, sleeping well, taking care of my people, and perfectly contented. . . . I would like to know now who it was that gave the order to arrest me and hang me. I was living peaceably there with my family under the shade of the trees, doing just what General Crook had told me I must do and trying to follow his advice. I want to know now who it was ordered me to be arrested. I was praying to the light and to the darkness, to God and to the sun, to let me live quietly there with my family. I don't know what the reason was that people should speak badly of me. . . .

Now, I am going to tell you something else. The Earth-Mother is listening to me and I hope that all may be so arranged that from now on there shall be no trouble and that we shall always have peace. . . . While living I want to live well. I know I have to die sometime, but even if the heavens were to fall on me, I want to do what is right. I think I am a good man, but in the papers all over the world they say I am a bad man; but it is a bad thing to say so about me. I never do wrong without a cause. Every day I am thinking, how am I to talk to you to make you believe what I say; and, I think, too, that you are thinking of what you are to say to me. There is one God looking down on us all. We are all children of the one God. God is listening to me. The sun, the darkness, the winds, are all listening to what we now say.

Geronimo, Apache

THE INDIAN WARRIOR

THE OLD MEN have told us that nothing here can last forever. They say that when men grow old and can no longer eat hard food, life is worth little. They tell us that everything we can see, except the earth and sky, changes a little even during a man's natural lifetime, and that when change comes to any created thing it must accept it, that it cannot fight, but must change. We do not know what may happen today, but let us act as though we were the Seven-stars [Big Dipper] in the sky that live forever. Go with me as far as you can, and I will go with you while there is breath in my body. Let us both remember there are two sights on our guns, and not shoot until we have seen them both. Let us shoot at a man's body where it sits on his horse, so that we shall not miss our marks altogether.

Plenty Coups, Crow

Geronimo (far right) and his warriors, 1886

THE INDIAN WARRIOR

YOUNG MEN, riding high-spirited horses whose hoofs scarcely touched the ground, would dash past us, and, showing off before the young women, race out of our sight. Then our mothers would talk among themselves, but so that we might hear. . . . "He is so brave, and so handsome." "Yes, and he has already counted coup and may marry when he chooses," another would boast. "Think of it!" another mother would exclaim. "He has seen but twenty snows! Ah-mmmmm!" Perhaps she would lay her hand over her mouth, which is a sign for astonishment. This talking between our mothers, firing us with determination to distinguish ourselves, made us wish we were men. It was always going on—this talking among our elders, both men and women—and we were ever listening. On the march, in the village, everywhere, there was praise in our ears for skill and daring. Our mothers talked before us of the deeds of other women's sons, and warriors told stories of the bravery and fortitude of other warriors until a listening boy would gladly die to have his name spoken by the chiefs in council, or even by the women in their lodges.

Plenty Coups, Crow

IN MY YOUTHFUL DAYS, I have seen large herds of buffalo on these prairies, and elk were found in every grove, but they are here no more, having gone towards the setting sun. For hundreds of miles no white man lived, but now trading posts and settlers are found here and there throughout the country, and in a few years the smoke from their cabins will be seen to ascend from every grove, and the prairie covered with their cornfields. . . . The red man must leave the land of his youth and find a new home in the far west. The armies of the whites are without number, like the sands of the sea, and ruin will follow all tribes that go to war with them.

Shabonee, Potawatomi

Chief Crane (left) and unidentified,
Potawatomi, c. 1860

Chief Joseph (Rolling Thunder),
Nez Perce, 1877

THE INDIAN WARRIOR

GOING ON THE WARPATH
You should give up
And (to) settle down
You should desire
And stop for good.

Sioux Song

ccc

IT WAS LONESOME, the leaving. Husband dead, friends buried or held prisoners. I felt that I was leaving all that I had but I did not cry. You know how you feel when you lose kindred and friends through sickness—death. You do not care if you die. With us it was worse. Strong men, well women and little children killed and buried. They had not done wrong to be so killed. We had only asked to be left in our own homes, the homes of our ancestors. Our going was with heavy hearts, broken spirits. But we would be free. . . . All lost, we walked silently on into the wintry night.

Wetatonmi, Nez Perce

ccc

I HAVE HEARD TALK AND TALK, but nothing is done. Good words do not last long unless they amount to something. Words do not pay for my dead people. They do not pay for my country, now overrun by white men. They do not protect my father's grave. They do not pay for all my horses and cattle. Good words will not give me back my children. . . . Good words will not give my people good health and stop them from dying. Good words will not get my people a home where they can live in peace and take care of themselves. I am tired of talk that comes to nothing. It makes my heart sick when I remember all the good words and the broken promises.

Chief Joseph (Rolling Thunder), Nez Perce

THE INDIAN WARRIOR

NOTHING HAPPENED after that. We just lived. There were no more war parties, no capturing of horses from the Piegans and the Sioux, no buffalo to hunt. There is nothing more to tell.

Two Leggings, Crow

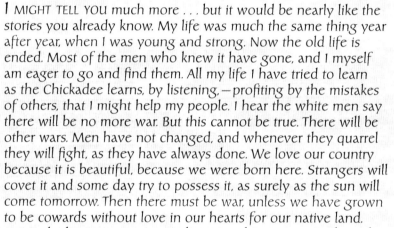

I MIGHT TELL YOU much more . . . but it would be nearly like the stories you already know. My life was much the same thing year after year, when I was young and strong. Now the old life is ended. Most of the men who knew it have gone, and I myself am eager to go and find them. All my life I have tried to learn as the Chickadee learns, by listening, — profiting by the mistakes of others, that I might help my people. I hear the white men say there will be no more war. But this cannot be true. There will be other wars. Men have not changed, and whenever they quarrel they will fight, as they have always done. We love our country because it is beautiful, because we were born here. Strangers will covet it and some day try to possess it, as surely as the sun will come tomorrow. Then there must be war, unless we have grown to be cowards without love in our hearts for our native land.

And whenever war comes between this country and another, your people will find my people pointing their guns with yours. My heart sings with pride when I think of the fighting my people, the red men of all tribes, did in this last great war [World War I]; and if ever the hands of my own people hold the rope that keeps this country's flag high in the air, it will never come down while an Absarokee [Crow] warrior lives.

Plenty Coups, Crow

Ernest Childers (right), Creek, receiving Medal of Honor from General Jacob L. Devers, 1944

Glen Douglas, Okanagan

Airman 1st Class
Lauren Tsosie, Navajo

Dr. Judy Peters,
Walpole Island Nation

Lt. Cody Ayon,
Cheyenne

Dan Akee, Navajo Code Talker

SPEAKERS

TRIBES

ARTISTS & PHOTOGRAPHERS

SOURCES

Annual Report of the Secretary of War on the Operations of the Department for the Fiscal Year Ending June 30, 1877, Vol. 1. Washington: U.S. Government Printing Office, 1877.

Ball, Eve. *In the Days of Victorio: Recollections of a Warm Springs Apache*. Tucson: University of Arizona Press, 1970.

Barrett, Stephen M., ed. *Geronimo's Story of His Life*. New York: Duffield & Company, 1906.

Bunzel, Ruth. *Zuni Texts*. New York: G. E. Stechert and Co., 1933.

Claiborne, John F. H. *Life and Times of Gen. Sam. Dale: The Mississippi Partisan*. New York: Harper & Brothers, 1860.

Courlander, Harold. *The Fourth World of the Hopis: The Epic Story of the Hopi Indians as Preserved in Their Legends and Traditions*. Albuquerque: University of New Mexico Press, 1971.

DeMallie, Raymond J., ed. *The Sixth Grandfather: Black Elk's Teachings Given to John G. Neihardt*. Lincoln: University of Nebraska Press, 1984.

Denig, Edwin T. "Indian Tribes of the Upper Missouri". Smithsonian Institution, Bureau of American Ethnology, Forty-sixth Annual Report 1928-29. Washington: U.S. Government Printing Office, 1930.

Densmore, Frances. *Chippewa Music—II*. Smithsonian Institution, Bureau of American Ethnology, Bulletin 53. Washington: U.S. Government Printing Office, 1913.

———. *Pawnee Music*. Smithsonian Institution, Bureau of American Ethnology, Bulletin 93. Washington: U.S. Government Printing Office, 1929.

———. *Teton Sioux Music*. Smithsonian Institution, Bureau of American Ethnology, Bulletin 61. Washington: U.S. Government Printing Office, 1918.

Donaldson, Thomas. "The George Catlin Indian Gallery in the U.S. National Museum". Annual Report of the Board of Regents of the Smithsonian Institution to July, 1885, Part 2. Washington: Government Printing Office, 1886.

Drake, Samuel G. *The Book of the Indians of North America: Comprising Details in the Lives of About Five Hundred Chiefs and Others, the Most Distinguished Among Them.* Boston: Josiah Drake, 1833.

Eastman, Charles A. *Indian Boyhood.* New York: McClure, Phillips & Co., 1902.

Ewers, John C. *The Horse in Blackfoot Indian Culture, with Comparative Material from Other Western Tribes.* Smithsonian Institution, Bureau of American Ethnology, Bulletin 159. Washington: U.S. Government Printing Office, 1955.

The Executive Documents of the Senate of the United States for the First Session of the Fifty-first Congress. Congressional Series of United States Public Documents, Volume 2686. Washington: U.S. Government Printing Office, 1890.

Goodrich, Samuel. *Lives of Celebrated American Indians.* New York: J. M. Allen, 1843.

Gordon, Hanford L. *The Feast of the Virgins and Other Poems.* Chicago: Laird & Lee, 1891.

Grinnell, George Bird. *The Fighting Cheyennes.* New York: Charles Scribner's Sons, 1915.

———. *Pawnee Hero Stories and Folk-Tales: With Notes on the Origin, Customs and Character of the Pawnee People.* New York: Charles Scribner's Sons, 1893.

Hardorff, Richard G. *Lakota Recollections of the Custer Fight: New Sources of Indian-Military History.* Lincoln: University of Nebraska Press, 1991.

Hazard, Samuel, ed. *Hazard's Register of Pennsylvania, Devoted to the Preservation of Facts and Document and Every Kind of Useful Information Respecting the State of Pennsylvania,* Vol. 8. Philadelphia: W. F. Geddes, 1832.

Holcombe, Robert I., ed. "A Sioux Story of the War: Chief Big Eagle's Story of the Sioux Outbreak of 1862." *Collections of the Minnesota Historical Society*, Vol. 6. St. Paul: The Pioneer Press Company, 1894.

Hunter, John D. *Memoirs of a Captivity Among the Indians of North America, from Childhood to the Age of Nineteen: With Anecdotes Descriptive of Their Manners and Customs.* London: Longman, Hurst, Orme, Brown, and Green, 1823.

Jefferson, Thomas. *Notes on the State of Virginia.* London: John Stockdale, 1787.

Johnson, W. Fletcher. *Life of Sitting Bull and History of the Indian War of 1890-91.* Philadelphia: Edgewood Publishing Company, 1891.

Joseph, Chief. "An Indian's Views of Indian Affairs". *North American Review.* Vol. 128, No. 269, April 1879.

Kendall's Expositor for 1843, Containing an Epitome of the Proceedings of Congress and Dissertations upon Currency, Exchanges, the Tariff, and Other Subjects, Vol. 3, 1843.

LaFlesche, Frances. *War Ceremony and Peace Ceremony of the Osage Indians.* Smithsonian Institution, Bureau of American Ethnology, Bulletin 101. Washington: U.S. Government Printing Office, 1939.

Linderman, Frank B. *American: The Life Story of a Great Indian: Plenty-coups, Chief of the Crows.* New York: John Day, 1930.

Lowie, R. H. *The Religion of the Crow Indians.* Anthropological Papers of the American Museum of Natural History, Vol. 25, Part 2. New York, 1922.

Marquis, Thomas B. *Wooden Leg: A Warrior Who Fought Custer.* Minneapolis: The Midwest Company, 1931.

Matson, Nehemiah. *Memories of Shaubena: With Incidents Relating to Indian Wars and the Early Settlement of the West.* Chicago: D. B. Cooke & Co, 1878.

McWhorter, Lucullus V. *Hear Me, My Chiefs! Nez Perce History and Legend.* Caldwell, ID: Caxton Press, 1952.

Nabokov, Peter. *Two Leggings: The Making of a Crow Warrior*. New York: Crowell, 1967.

Neihardt, John G. *Black Elk Speaks: Being the Life Story of a Holy Man of the Ogalala Sioux*. New York: William Morrow & Company, 1932.

Niles' Weekly Register, Vol. 9, No. 7. Baltimore, Saturday October 14, 1815.

Papers Relating to Talks and Councils Held with the Indians in Dakota and Montana in the Years 1866-1869. Washington: U.S. Government Printing Office, 1910.

Patterson, John B., ed. *Life of Ma-Ka-Tai-Me-She-Kia-Kiak, or Black Hawk*. Boston: Russell, Odiorne & Metcalf 1834.

Paul, R. Eli, ed. *Autobiography of Red Cloud: War Leader of the Oglalas*. Helena: Montana Historical Society Press, 1997.

Proud, Robert. *The History of Pennsylvania*, Vol. 2. Philadelphia: Zachariah Poulson, 1797.

Speech of Corn Plant, Half Town, and Big Tree to the President of the United States. *The American Magazine, or, Universal Magazine*, Part 1. Philadelphia: M. Carey, 1792.

Speech of Tecumseh, August 20, 1810. In *Papers of William Henry Harrison, 1800-1815*. Reel 4, frame 156, microfilm edition. Edited by Douglas E. Clanin et al. Indianapolis: Indiana Historical Society, 1999.

Sprague, John T. *The Origin, Progress, and Conclusion of the Florida War*. New York: D. Appleton & Company, 1848.

Standing Bear, Luther. *Land of the Spotted Eagle*. Boston: Houghton Mifflin, 1933.

Steward, Julian H. *Two Paiute Autobiographies*. Berkeley: University of California Press, 1934.

Stone, William L. *Life of Joseph Brant—Thayendanegea*, Vol. 2. New York: Alexander V. Blake 1838.

————. *The Life and Times of Red-Jacket or Sa-go-ye-wat-ha*. New York: Wiley and Putnam, 1841.

Thatcher, Benjamin B. *Indian Biography, Or An Historical Account of Those Individuals Who Have Been Distinguished Among the North American Natives as Orators, Warriors, Statesmen, and Other Remarkable Characters*, Vol. 2. New. York: J. & J. Harper, 1832.

Underhill, Ruth. *Singing for Power: The Song Magic of the Papago Indians of Southern Arizona*. Berkeley, University of California Press, 1938.

The United States Army and Navy Journal, and Gazette of the Regular and Volunteer Forces, Vol 5, 1867-68. New York: Publication Office, 1868.

Thirty-seventh Annual Report of the Bureau of American Ethnology to the Secretary of the Smithsonian Institution, 1915-16. Washington: U.S. Government Printing Office, 1923.

Vestal, Stanley. *Warpath: The True Story of the Fighting Sioux Told in a Biography of Chief White Bull*. Boston: Houghton Mifflin, 1934.

Victor, Frances F. *Eleven Years in the Rocky Mountains and Life on the Frontier*. Hartford, CT: Columbian Book Company, 1877.

Walker, James. *Lakota Belief and Ritual*. Edited by Raymond J. DeMallie & Elaine A. Jahner. Lincoln: University of Nebraska Press, 1980.

BIOGRAPHICAL NOTES

Michael Oren Fitzgerald is the author and editor of over twenty books that have received more than thirty awards, including the ForeWord Book of the Year Award, the Ben Franklin Award, and two USA Best Book Awards. More than ten of Michael's books, along with two documentary films he produced, are used in high-school or university classes. He previously taught the Religious Traditions of the North American Indians at Indiana University. His works include *Indian Spirit, The Spirit of Indian Women, Spirit of the Earth: Indian Voices on Nature, The Essential Charles Eastman,* and *Living in Two Worlds: The American Indian Experience.* Michael lives with his wife in Bloomington, Indiana.

Joseph A. Fitzgerald studied Comparative Religion at Indiana University, where he also earned a Doctor of Jurisprudence degree. A recipient of the Ben Franklin Award and numerous other awards, Joseph has edited eleven books on diverse themes in world religion, culture, and philosophy. His works include *The Cheyenne Indians: Their History and Lifeways, Illustrated, World of the Teton Sioux Indians: Their Music, Life & Culture,* and *Spirit of the Earth: Indian Voices on Nature.*

Charles Trimble was born and reared on the Pine Ridge Indian Reservation in South Dakota. After receiving his B.F.A. from the University of South Dakota, he enlisted in the U.S. Army in 1957 and was honorably discharged in 1960. He served in Germany as an Infantry Operations Intelligence Specialist. Following service in the Army, he did further studies in journalism on the GI Bill at the University of Colorado. He went on to become a national leader in Indian affairs. In 1969 he was principal founder of the American Indian Press Association, and served as the organization's Executive Director until 1972, when he was elected Executive Director of the National Congress of American Indians. Charles was inducted into the South Dakota Hall of Fame in 2013 and is an enrolled member of the Oglala Sioux tribe. The author of *Iyeska,* he is now retired and lives in Omaha, Nebraska, with his wife, Anne.

Other American Indian Titles by World Wisdom

All Our Relatives: Traditional Native American Thoughts about Nature
compiled and illustrated by Paul Goble, 2005

Black Elk, Lakota Visionary: The Oglala Holy Man & Sioux Tradition
by Harry Oldmeadow, 2018

The Boy and His Mud Horses: And Other Stories from the Tipi
compiled and illustrated by Paul Goble, 2010

The Cheyenne Indians: Their History and Lifeways
by George Bird Grinnell, edited by Joseph A. Fitzgerald, 2008

Children of the Tipi: Life in the Buffalo Days
edited by Michael Oren Fitzgerald, 2013

Custer's Last Battle: Red Hawk's Account of the Battle of the Little Bighorn
compiled and illustrated by Paul Goble, 2013

The Earth Made New: Plains Indian Stories of Creation
compiled and illustrated by Paul Goble, 2009

The Essential Charles Eastman (Ohiyesa)
edited by Michael Oren Fitzgerald, 2007

The Feathered Sun: Plains Indians in Art and Philosophy
by Frithjof Schuon, 1990

The Gospel of the Redman: Commemorative Edition
compiled by Ernest Thompson Seton and Julia M. Seton, 2005

Horse Raid: The Making of a Warrior
compiled and illustrated by Paul Goble, 2014

The Hunter's Promise
by Joseph Bruchac, illustrated by Bill Farnsworth, 2015

The Image Taker: The Selected Stories and Photographs of Edward S. Curtis
edited by Gerald Hasuman and Bob Kapoun, 2009

Indian Spirit: Revised and Enlarged
edited by Judith and Michael Oren Fitzgerald, 2006

Living in Two Worlds: The American Indian Experience
by Charles Eastman, edited by Michael Oren Fitzgerald, 2010

The Man Who Dreamed of Elk-Dogs: & Other Stories from the Tipi
compiled and illustrated by Paul Goble, 2012

Native Spirit: The Sun Dance Way
by Thomas Yellowtail, edited by Michael Oren Fitzgerald, 2007

The Otter, the Spotted Frog, and the Great Flood
by Gerald Hausman, illustrated by Ramon Shiloh, 2013

Red Cloud's War: Brave Eagle's Account of the Fetterman Fight
compiled and illustrated by Paul Goble, 2015

The Spirit of Indian Women
edited by Judith and Michael Oren Fitzgerald, 2005

Spirit of the Earth: Indian Voices on Nature
edited by Joseph and Michael Oren Fitzgerald, 2017

*The Spiritual Legacy of the American Indian: Commemorative Edition
with Letters While Living with Black Elk*
by Joseph Epes Brown, 2007

The Thunder Egg
by Tim Myers, illustrated by Winfield Coleman, 2015

Tipi: Home of the Nomadic Buffalo Hunters
compiled and illustrated by Paul Goble, 2007

Whispers of the Wolf by Pauline Ts'o, 2015

The Women Who Lived with Wolves: And Other Stories from the Tipi
compiled and illustrated by Paul Goble, 2011

World of the Teton Sioux Indians: Their Music, Life & Culture
by Frances Densmore, edited by Joseph A. Fitzgerald, 2016

Films about American Indian Spirituality

Native Spirit & The Sun Dance Way
produced by Michael Oren Fitzgerald, directed by Jennifer Casey, 2007

About This Book

"*Spirit of the Indian Warrior* is a wonderful work by award-winning writers Michael Oren Fitzgerald and Joseph A. Fitzgerald. They have provided the profound words by Indian warriors and leaders regarding warfare and the reasons Indians went to war. The current comment used today to our military, 'thank you for your service,' is most appropriately applied to Indian nations and their struggles to exist. The book is beautifully illustrated and also contains photographs of contemporary Indian armed service men and women. Both general readers and serious students of Native American history will find this book an enjoyable and thought-provoking experience."

—**Raymond Wilson**, Professor Emeritus of History, Fort Hays State University, and author of *Ohiyesa: Charles A. Eastman, Santee Sioux*

"As witnessed by the sun, earth, and winds, whether during peace or warfare, the voices of seasoned statesmen echo to us in *Spirit of the Indian Warrior*. Their words manifest humility and gallantry against the onslaught of radical change invading their homelands. In photographs, their eyes gaze with a haunting calmness, mirroring the steadfastness and fidelity embodied in a warrior code grounded upon honor and truth. Their vision of the public good gives perseverance to our own way of life."

—**Vivian Arviso Deloria**, President of the Navajo Nation Women's Commission and former Executive Director of Education for the Navajo Nation